INDEX

Foreword

"The Babylonian Story of the Deluge and the Epic of Gilgamish is a collection of two ancient texts from Babylonian literature that have had a profound impact on the history of human thought and culture. The first text, the Poem of Atrahasis, tells the story of a great flood sent by the gods to punish humanity for their noise and overpopulation. The second text, the Epic of Gilgamesh, is one of the oldest works of literature in the world, dating back over 4,000 years. It tells the story of the semi-divine king Gilgamesh, who sets out on a journey to find the secret of immortality.

The Poem of Atrahasis is a powerful and moving account of a catastrophic event that has been depicted in many cultures throughout history, including the biblical story of the flood in the book of Genesis. This Babylonian version provides a unique perspective on the nature of divine punishment and the resilience of human survival. The story of Atrahasis and his family who survive the flood is a reminder of the human capacity for hope and determination in the face of adversity.

The Epic of Gilgamesh is a rich and complex work that explores themes of mortality, friendship, and the search for meaning in life. The story of Gilgamesh's journey to find immortality is a timeless tale of human aspiration and the quest for eternal life. The epic also includes powerful reflections on the nature of friendship and the importance of community, as well as the ultimate futility of trying to escape death.

The translations and annotations in this edition of The Babylonian Story of the Deluge and the Epic of Gilgamish are the result of many years of scholarly research and provide a clear and accessible introduction to these ancient texts. These texts are important not only for their historical significance but also for the timeless wisdom and insight they offer about the human condition. This edition of The Babylonian Story of the Deluge and the Epic of Gilgamish is a must-read for anyone interested in the history of literature, mythology, and the human experience."

J.O.P

The Discovery Of The Tablets At Nineveh By Layard, Rassam And Smith

IN 1845-47, and again in 1849-51, Mr. (later Sir) A. H. Layard carried out a series of excavations among the ruins of the ancient city of Nineveh, "that great city, wherein are more than sixteen thousand persons that cannot discern between their right hand and their left; and *also* much cattle" (Jonah iv, ii). Its ruins lie on the left or east bank of the Tigris, exactly opposite the town of At-Mawsil, or Môsul, which was founded by the Sassanians and marks the site of Western Nineveh. At first Layard thought that these ruins were not those of Nineveh, which he placed at Nimrûd, about 20 miles downstream, but of one of the other cities that were builded by Asshur (*see* Gen. X, 11, 12). Thanks, however, to Christian, Roman and Muhammadan tradition, there is no room for doubt about it, and the site of Nineveh has always been known. The fortress which the Arabs built there in the seventh century was known as "Kal'at Ninawï," *i.e.*, "Nineveh Castle," for many centuries, and all the Arab geographers agree in saying that the mounds opposite Môsul contain the ruins of the palaces and walls of Nineveh. And few of them fail to mention that close by them is "Tall Nabi Yûnis," *i.e.*, the Hill from which the Prophet Jonah preached repentance to the inhabitants of Nineveh, that "exceeding great city of three days' journey" (Jonah iii, 3). Local tradition also declares that the prophet was buried in the Hill, and his supposed tomb is shown there to this day.

The Walls And Palaces Of Nineveh

The situation of the ruins of the palaces of Nineveh is well shown by the accompanying reproduction of the plan of the city made by Commander Felix Jones, I.N. The remains of the older palaces built by Sargon II (B.C. 722-705), Sennacherib (B.C. 705-681), and Esarhaddon (B.C. 681-669) lie under the hill called Nabi Yûnis, and those of the palaces and other buildings of Asshur-bani-pal (B.C. 681-626) under the mound which is known locally as "Tall al-'Armûshîyah," *i.e.*, "The "Hill of 'Armûsh," and "Kuyûnjik." The latter name is said to be derived from two Turkish words meaning "many sheep," in allusion to the large flocks of sheep that find their pasture on and about the mound in the early spring. These two great mounds lie close to the remains of the great west wall of Nineveh, which in the time of the last Assyrian Empire may have been washed by the waters of the river Tigris.[1] The river Khausur, or Khoser, divides the area of Nineveh into two parts, and passing close to the southern end of Kuyûnjik empties itself into the Tigris. The ruins of the walls of Nineveh show that the east wall was 16,000 feet long, the north wall 7,000 feet long, the west wall 13,600 feet, and the south wall 3,000 feet; its circuit was about 13,200 yards or 7½ miles.

First Discovery Of The Royal Library At Nineveh

In the spring of 1850 Layard, assisted by Mr. H. Rassam, continued the excavation of the "South West Palace" at Kuyûnjik. In one part of the building he found two small chambers, opening into each other, which be called the "chamber of records," or "the house of the rolls." He gave them this name because "to the height of a foot or more from the floor they were entirely filled with inscribed baked clay tablets and fragments of tablets. Some tablets were complete, but by far the larger number of them had been broken up into many fragments, probably by the falling in of the roof and upper parts of the walls of the buildings when the city was pillaged and set on fire by the Medes and Babylonians. The tablets that were kept in these chambers numbered many thousands. Besides those that were found in them by Layard, large numbers have been dug out all along the corridor which passed the chambers and led to the river, and a considerable number were kicked on to the river front by the feet of the terrified fugitives from the palace when it was set on fire. The tablets found by Layard were of different sizes; the largest were rectangular, flat on one side and convex on the other, and measured about 9 ins. by 6½ ins., and the smallest were about an inch square. The importance of this "find" was not sufficiently recognized at the time, for the tablets, which were thought to be decorated pottery, were thrown into baskets and sent down the river loose on rafts to Basrah, whence they were despatched to England on a British man-of-war. During their transport from Nineveh to England they suffered more damage from want of packing than they had suffered from the wrath of the Medes. Among the complete tablets that were found in the two chambers several had colophons inscribed or scratched upon them, and when these were deciphered by Rawlinson, Hincks and Oppert a few years later, it became evident that they had formed part of the Library of the TEMPLE OF NEBO AT NINEVEH.

Nebo And His Library At Nineveh

Nothing is known of the early history of the Library[2] of the Temple of Nebo at Nineveh, but there is little doubt that it was in existence in the reign of Sargon II. Authorities differ in their estimate of the attributes that were assigned to Nebo (*Nabu*) in Pre-Babylonian times, and "cannot decide whether he was a water-god, or a fire-god, or a corn-god, but he was undoubtedly associated with Marduk, either as his son or as a fellow-god. It is certain that as early as B.C. 2000 he was regarded as one of the "Great Gods" of Babylonia, and in the fourteenth century B.C. his cult was already established in Assyria.

He had a temple at Nimrûd in the ninth century B.C., and King Adad-nirari (B.C. 811-783) set up six statues in it to the honour of the god; two of these statues are now in the British Museum. The same Adad-nirari also repaired the Nebo temple at Nineveh. Under the last Assyrian Empire Nebo was believed to possess the wisdom of all the gods, and to be the "All-wise " and "All-knowing."

He was the inventor of all the arts and sciences, and the source of inspiration in wise and learned men, and he was the divine scribe and past master of all the mysteries connected with literature and the art of writing (*dup-sharrute*). Ashur-bani-pal addresses him as "Nebo, the mighty son, the director of the whole of heaven and of earth, holder of the tablet, bearer of the writing-reed of the tablet of destiny, lengthener of days, vivifier of the dead, stablisher of light for the men who are troubled" (see Tablet, RM. 132).

In the reign of Sargon II the Temple of Nebo at Kuyûnjik[3] was repaired, and probably at that time a library was housed in it. Layard found some of the remains of Nebo's Library in the South West Palace, but it must have been transferred thither, for the temple of Nebo lay farther north, near the south corner of Ashur-bani-pal's palace. Nebo's temple at Nineveh bore the same name as his very ancient temple at Borsippa (the modem Birs-i-Nimrûd), viz., "E-ZIDA."

Discovery Of The Palace Library Of Ashur-Bani-Pal

In the spring of 1851 Layard was obliged to close his excavations for want of funds, and he returned to England with Rassam, leaving all the northern half of the great mound of Kuyûnjik unexcavated. He resigned his position as Director of Excavations to the Trustees of the British Museum, and Colonel (later Sir) H. C. Rawlinson, Consul-General at Baghdâd, undertook to direct any further excavations that it might be possible to carry out later on. During the summer the Trustees received a further grant from Parliament for excavations in Assyria, and they dispatched Rassam to finish the exploration of Kuyûnjik, knowing that the lease of the mound of Kuyûnjik for excavation purposes which he had obtained from its owner had several years to run. When Rassam arrived at Môsul in 1852, and was collecting his men for work, he discovered that Rawlinson, who knew nothing about the lease of the mound which Rassam held, had given the French Consul, M. Place, permission to excavate the northern half of the mound, *i.e.*, that part of it which he was most anxious to excavate for the British Museum.

He protested, but in vain, and, finding that M. Place intended to hold Rawlinson to his word, devoted himself to clearing out part of the South West Palace which Layard had attacked in 1850. Meanwhile M. Place was busily occupied with the French excavations at Khorsabad, a mound which contained the ruins of the great palace of Sargon II, and had no time to open up excavations at Kuyûnjik.

In this way a year passed, and as M. Place made no sign that he was going to excavate at Kuyûnjik, and Rassam's time for returning to England was drawing near, the owner of the mound, who was anxious to get the excavations finished so that he might again graze his flocks on the mound, urged Rassam to get to work in spite of Rawlinson's agreement with M. Place. He and Rassam made arrangements to excavate the northern part of the mound clandestinely and by night, and on 20th December, 1853, the work began.

On the first night nothing of importance was found; on the second night the men uncovered a portion of a large bas-relief; and on the third night a huge mass of earth collapsed revealing a very fine bas-relief, sculptured with a scene representing Ashur-bani-pal standing in his chariot. The news of the discovery was quickly carried to all parts of the neighbourhood, and as it was impossible to keep the diggings secret any longer, the work was continued openly and by day.

The last-mentioned bas-relief was one of the series that lined the chamber, which was 50 feet long and 15 feet wide, and illustrated a royal lion hunt. This series, that is to say, all of it that the fire which destroyed the palace had spared, is now in the British Museum (see the Gallery of the Assyrian Saloon).[4]

Whilst the workmen were clearing out the Chamber of the Lion Hunt they came across several heaps of inscribed baked clay tablets of "all shapes and sizes," which resembled in general appearance the tablets that Layard had found in the South West Palace the year before. There were no remains with them, or near them, that suggested they had been arranged systematically and stored in the Chamber of the Lion Hunt, and it seems as if they had been brought there from another place and thrown down hastily, for nearly all of them were broken into small pieces.

As some of them bore traces of having been exposed to great heat they must have been in that chamber during the burning of the palace. When the tablets were brought to England and were examined by Rawlinson, it was found from the information supplied by the colophons that they formed a part of the great PRIVATE LIBRARY OF ASHUR-BANI-PAL, which that king kept in his palace. The tablets found by Layard in 1850 and by Rassam in 1853 form the unique and magnificent collection of cuneiform tablets in the British Museum, which is now commonly known as the "Kuyûnjik Collection." The approximate number of the inscribed baked clay tablets and fragments that have come from Kuyûnjik and are now in the British Museum is 25,073. It is impossible to over-estimate their importance and value from religious, historical and literary points of view; besides this, they have supplied the material for the decipherment of cuneiform inscriptions in the Assyrian, Babylonian and Sumerian languages, and form the foundation of the science of Assyriology which has been built up with such conspicuous success during the last 70 years.

Ashur-Bani-Pal, Book-Collector And Patron Of Learning

Ashur-bani-pal (the Asnapper of Ezra iv, 10) succeeded his father Esarhaddon B.C. 669, and at a comparatively early period of his reign he seems to have devoted himself to the study of the history of his country, and to the making of a great Private Library. The tablets that have come down to us prove not only that he was as great a benefactor of the Library of the Temple of Nebo as any of his predecessors, but that he was himself an educated man, a lover of learning, and a patron of the literary folk of his day. In the introduction to his Annals, as found inscribed on his great ten-sided prism in the British Museum, he tells us how he took up his abode in the Crown Prince's dwelling from which Sermacherib and Esarhaddon had ruled the Assyrian Empire, and in describing his own education he says:

"I, Ashur-bani-pal, within it (*i.e.*, the palace) understood the wisdom of Nebo, all the art of writing of every craftsman, of every kind, I made myself master of them all (*i.e.*, of the various kinds of writing)."

These words suggest that Ashur-bani-pal could not only read cuneiform texts, but could write like a skilled scribe, and that he also understood all the details connected with the craft of making and baking tablets. Having determined to form a Library in his palace he set to work in a systematic manner to collect literary works. He sent scribes to ancient seats of learning, *e.g.*, Ashur, Babylon, Cuthah, Nippur, Akkad, Erech, to make copies of the ancient works that were preserved there, and when the copies came to Nineveh he either made transcripts of them himself, or caused his scribes to do so for the Palace Library. In any case he collated the texts himself and revised them before placing them in his Library. The appearance of the tablets from his Library suggests that he established a factory in which the clay was cleaned and kneaded and made into homogeneous, well-shaped tablets, and a kiln in which they were baked, after they had been inscribed. The uniformity of the script upon them is very remarkable, and texts with mistakes in them are rarely found. How the tablets were arranged in the Library is not known, but certainly groups were catalogued, and some tablets were labelled.[5] Groups of tablets were arranged in numbered series, with "catch lines," the first tablet of the series giving the first line of the second tablet, the second tablet giving the first line of the third tablet, and so on.

Extract from a List of Signs with Sumerian and Assyrian values. From Rawlinson, *Cuneiform Inscriptions of Western Asia*, Vol. II, Plate I, ll. 155–168.

Ashur-bani-pal was greatly interested in the literature of the Sumerians, *i.e.*, the non-Semitic people who occupied Lower Babylonia about B.C. 3500 and later. He and his scribes made bilingual lists of signs and words and objects of all classes and kinds, all of which are of priceless value to the modem student of the Sumerian and Assyrian languages. Annexed is an extract from a List of Signs with Sumerian and Assyrian values. The signs of which the meanings are given are in the middle column; the Sumerian values are given in the column to the left, and their meanings in Assyrian in the column to the right. To many of his copies of Sumerian hymns, incantations, magical formulas, etc., Ashur-bani-pal caused interlinear translations to be added in Assyrian, and of such bilingual documents the following extract from a text relating to the Seven Evil Spirits will serve as a specimen. The 1st, 3rd, 5th, etc., lines are written in Sumerian, and the 2nd, 4th, 6th, etc., lines in Assyrian.

Extract from a tablet containing a text relating to the Seven Evil Spirits, written in the Sumerian language, with an interlinear translation in Assyrian. From Rawlinson, *Cuneiform Inscription of Western Asia*, Vol. IV, Plate XV, Obverse, ll. 33–46 (K. III—K. 2754).

Most of the tablets from Kuyûnjik end with colophons, which can be divided broadly into two classes. One of these is the short note, frequently impressed by a stamp, which reads simply "Palace of Ashur-bani-pal, king of all, king of Assyria" (see the tablet illustrated on p. 22). The longer forms of colophon were added by the scribes who had written the whole tablet. Of these longer colophons there are several versions, each of which seems to have been appropriated to a particular class of texts. Two of the most interesting are here appended; they reveal a distinction between tablets belonging to the Palace Library and those preserved in the Temple of Nebo.

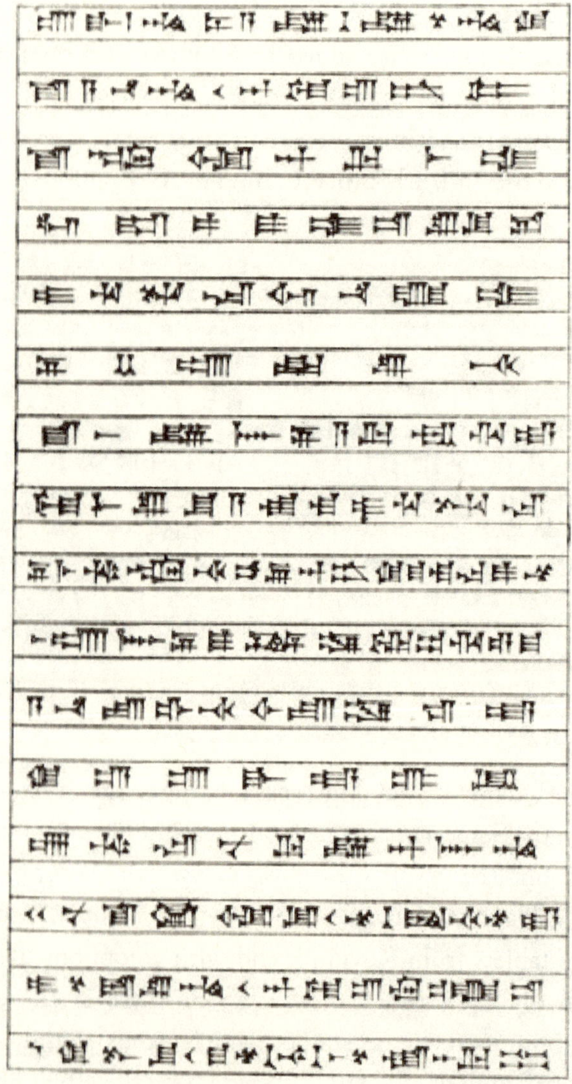

Colophon of a tablet from the Palace Library of Ashur-bani-pal containing incantations in the Sumerian language, with interlinear translations in Assyrian. For an English rendering see following page. From Rawlinson, *Cuneiform Inscriptions of Western Asia*, Vol. IV, Plate VI, col. 6 (K. 4870).

I. Colophon of the Tablets of the Palace Library. (K. 4870.)

1. Palace of Ashur-bani-pal, king of all, king of the country of Assyria,

2. who trusteth in the god Ashur and the goddess Ninlil,

3. on whom the god Nebo (Nabû) and the goddess Tashmetu

4. have bestowed all-hearing ears

5. and who has eyes that are clearsighted.

6. The finest results of the art of writing

7. which, among the kings who have gone before,

8. no one ever acquired that craft,

9. the wisdom of Nebo [expressed in] rows (?) of writing, of every form,

10. on tablets I wrote, collated and revised,

11. [and] for examination and reading

12. in my palace I placed—[6]

13. the prince who knoweth the light of the king of the gods, Ashur.'

14. Whosoever shall carry [them] off, or his name side by side with mine

15. shall write, may Ashur and Ninlil, wrathfully, furiously

16. sweep away, and his name and his seed destroy in the land.

2. COLOPHON OF THE TABLETS OF THE LIBRARY OF NEBO. (Rm. 132.)

1. To Nebo, the mighty son, director of the whole of heaven and of earth,

2. holder of the tablet, bearer of the writing reed of the tablet of destinies,

3. lengthener of days, vivifier of the dead, stablisher of light for the men who are troubled,

4. the great lord, his lord; Ashur-bani-pal, the prince, the favourite of the gods Ashur, Bêl and Nebo,

5. the shepherd, the maintainer of the holy places of the great gods, stablisher of their revenues,

6. son of Esarhaddon, king of all, king of Assyria,

7. grandson of Sennacherib, king of all, king of Assyria,

8. for the life of his soul, length of his days, [and] well-being of his posterity,

9. to make permanent the foundation of his royal throne, to hear his supplications,

10. to receive his petitions, to deliver into his hands the rebellious.

11. The wisdom of Ea, the chanter's art, the secrets of the sages,

12. what is composed for the contentment of the heart of the great gods,

13. I wrote upon tablets, I collated, I revised

14. according to originals of the lands of Ashur and Akkad,

15. and I placed in the Library of E-zida, the temple of Nebo my lord, which is in Nineveh.

16. O Nebo, lord of the whole of heaven and of earth, look upon that Library joyfully for years (*i.e.*, for ever).

17. On Ashur-bani-pal, the chief, the worshipper of thy divinity, daily bestow grace,

18. his life decree, so that he may exalt thy great godhead.

The tablets from both Libraries when unbroken vary in size from 15 inches by 85/8 inches to 1 inch by 7/8 inch, and they are usually about 1 inch thick. In shape they are rectangular, the obverse being flat and the reverse slightly convex. Contract tablets, letter tablets and "case" tablets are very much smaller, and resemble small pillows in shape. The principal subjects dealt with in the tablets are history, annalistic or summaries, letters, despatches, reports, oracles, prayers, contracts, deeds of sale of land, produce, cattle, slaves, agreements, dowries, bonds for interest (with impressions of seals, and fingernails, or nail marks), chronography, chronology, canons of eponyms, divination (by astrology, the entrails of victims, oil, casual events, dreams, and symptoms), charms, spells, incantations, mythology, legends, grammar, law, geography, etc.[7]

George Smith's Discovery Of The Epic Of Gilgamish And The Story Of The Deluge

The mass of tablets which had been discovered by Layard and Rassam at Nineveh came to the British Museum in 1854-5, and their examination by Rawlinson and Norris began very soon after. Mr. Bowler, a skilful draughtsman and copyist of tablets, whom Rawlinson employed in making transfers of copies of cuneiform texts for publication by lithography, rejoined a considerable number of fragments of bilingual lists, syllabaries, etc., which were published in the second volume of the *Cuneiform Inscriptions of Western Asia*, in 1866. In that year the Trustees of the British Museum employed George Smith to assist Rawlinson in sorting, classifying and rejoining fragments, and a comprehensive examination of the collection by him began. His personal interest in Assyriology was centred upon historical texts, especially those which threw any light on the Bible Narrative. But in the course of his search for stories of the campaigns of Sargon II, Sennacherib, Esarhaddon and Ashur-bani-pal, he discovered among other important documents (1) a series of portions of tablets which give the adventures of Gilgamish, an ancient king of Erech; (2) an account of the Deluge, which is supplied by the Eleventh Tablet of the Legend of Gilgamish (in more than one version); (3) a detailed description of the Creation; (4) the Legend of the Descent of Ishtar into Hades in quest of Tammuz. The general meaning of the texts was quite clear, but there were many gaps in them, and it was not until December, 1872, that George Smith published his description of the Legend of Gilgamish, and a translation of the "Chaldean Account of the Deluge." The interest which his paper evoked was universal, and the proprietors of *The Daily Telegraph* advocated that Smith should be at once dispatched to Nineveh to search for the missing fragments of tablets which would fill up the gaps in his texts, and generously offered to contribute 1,000 guineas towards the cost of the excavations. The

Trustees accepted the offer and gave six months' leave of absence to Smith, who left London in January, and arrived in Môsul in March, 1873. In the following May he recovered from Kuyûnjik a fragment that contained "the greater portion of seventeen lines of inscription belonging to the first column of the Chaldean account of the Deluge, and fitting into the only place where there was a serious blank in the story."[8] During the excavations which Smith carried out at Kuyûnjik in 1873 and 1874 he recovered many fragments of tablets, the texts of which enabled him to complete his description of the contents of the Twelve Tablets of the Legend of Gilgamish which included his translation of the story of the Deluge. Unfortunately Smith died of hunger and sickness near Aleppo in 1876, and he was unable to revise his early work, and to supplement it with the information which he had acquired during his latest travels in Assyria and Babylonia. Thanks to the excavations which were carried on at Kuyûnjik by the Trustees of the British Museum after his untimely death, several hundreds of tablets and fragments have been recovered, and many of these have been rejoined to the tablets of the older collection. By the careful study and investigation of the old and new material Assyriologists have, during the last forty years, been enabled to restore and complete many passages in the Legends of Gilgamish and the Flood. It now seems that the Legend of the Flood had not originally any connection with the Legend of Gilgamish, and that it was introduced into it by a late editor or redactor of the Legend, probably in order to complete the number of the Twelve Tablets on which it was written in the time of Ashur-bani-pal.

The Legend Of The Deluge In Babylonia

In the introduction to his paper on the "Chaldean Account of the Deluge," which Smith read in December, 1872, and published in 1873, he stated that the Assyrian text which he had found on Ashur-bani-pal's tablets was copied from an archetype at Erech in Lower Babylonia. This archetype was, he thought, "either written in, or translated into Semitic Babylonian, to at a very early period," and although he could not assign a date to it, he adduced a number of convincing proofs in support of his opinion. The language in which he assumed the Legend to have been originally composed was known to him under the name of "Accadian," or "Akkadian," but is now called "Sumerian." Recent research has shown that his view on this point was correct on the whole. But there is satisfactory proof available to show that versions or recensions of the Legend of the Deluge and of the Epic of Gilgamish existed both in Sumerian and Babylonian, as early as B.C. 2000. The discovery has been made of a fragment of a tablet with a small portion of the Babylonian version of the Legend of the Deluge inscribed upon it, and dated in a year which is the equivalent of the 11th year of Ammisaduga, *i.e.*, about B.C. 1800.[2] And in the Museum at Philadelphia[10] is preserved half of a tablet which when whole contained a complete copy of a Sumerian version of the Legend, and must have been written about the same date. The fragment of the tablet written in the reign of Ammisaduga is of special importance because the colophon shows that the tablet to which it belonged was the second of a series, and that this series was not that of the Epic of Gilgamish, and from this we learn that in B.C. 2000 the Legend of the Deluge did not form the XIth Tablet of the Epic of Gilgamish, as it did in the reign of Ashur-bani-pal, or earlier. The Sumerian version is equally important, though from another point of view, for the contents and position of the portion of it that remains on the half of the tablet mentioned above make it certain that already at this early period there were several versions of the Legend of the Deluge current in the Sumerian language. The fact is that the Legend of the Deluge was then already so old in Mesopotamia that the scribes added to or abbreviated the text at will, and treated the incidents recorded in it according to local or popular taste, tradition and prejudice. There seems to be no evidence that proves conclusively that the Sumerian version is older than the Semitic, or that the latter was translated direct from the former version. It is probable that both the Sumerians and the Semites, each in their own way, attempted to commemorate an appalling disaster of unparalleled magnitude, the knowledge of which, through tradition, was common to both peoples. It is, at all events, well known that the Sumerians regarded the Deluge as an historic event, which they were, practically, able to date, for some of their records contain lists of kings who reigned before the Deluge, though it must be confessed that the lengths assigned to their reigns are incredible. After their rule it is expressly noted that the Flood occurred, and that, when it passed away, kingship came down again from on high.

It is not too much to assume that the original event commemorated in the Legend of the Deluge was a serious and prolonged inundation or flood in Lower Babylonia, which was accompanied by great loss of life and destruction of property. The Babylonian versions state that this inundation or flood was caused by rain, but passages in some of them suggest that the effects of the rainstorm were intensified bv other physical happenings connected with the earth, of a most destructive character. The Hebrews also, as we may see from the Bible, had alternative views as to the cause of the Deluge. According to one, rain fell upon the earth for forty days and forty nights (Gen. vii, 12), and according to the other the Deluge came because "all the fountains of the great deep" were broken up, and "the flood-gates of heaven were opened" (Gen. vii, ii). The latter view suggests that the rain flood was joined by the waters of the sea. Later tradition, derived partly from Babylonian and partly from Hebrew sources, asserts, *e.g.,* in the *Cave of Treasures,* a Syriac treatise composed probably at Edessa about the fifth or sixth century A.D., that when Noah had entered the Ark and the door was shut "the floodgates of the heavens were opened it and the foundations of the earth were rent asunder," and that "the ocean, that great sea which surroundeth the whole world, poured forth its floods. And whilst the floodgates of heaven were open, and the foundations of the earth were rent asunder, the storehouses of the winds burst their bolts, and storms and whirlwinds swept forth, and ocean roared and hurled its floods upon the earth." The ark was steered over the waters by an angel who acted as pilot, and when that had come to rest on the mountains of Kardô (Ararat), "God commanded the waters and they became separated from each other. The celestial waters were taken up and ascended to their own place above the heavens whence they came.

The waters which had risen up from the earth returned to the lowermost abyss, and those which belonged to the ocean returned to the innermost part thereof."[11] Many authorities seeking to find a foundation of fact for the Legend of the Deluge in Mesopotamia have assumed that the rain-flood was accompanied either by an earthquake or a tidal-wave, or by both. There is no doubt that the cities of Lower Babylonia were nearer the sea in the Sumerian Period than they are at present, and it is a generally accepted view that the head of the Persian Gulf lay farther to the north at that time. A cyclone coupled with a tidal wave is a sufficient base for any of the forms of the Legend now known.

A comparison of the contents of the various Sumerian and Babylonian versions of the Deluge that have come down to us shows us that they are incomplete.

And as none of them tells so connected and full a narrative of the prehistoric shipbuilder as Berosus, a priest of Bêl, the great god of Babylon, it seems that the Mesopotamian scribes were content to copy the Legend in an abbreviated form. Berosus, it is true, is not a very ancient authority, for he was not born until the reign of Alexander the Great, but he was a learned man and was well acquainted with the

Babylonian language, and with the ancient literature of his country, and he wrote a history of Babylonia, some fragments of which have been preserved to us in the works of Alexander Polyhistor, Eusebius, and others. The following is a version of the fragment which describes the flood that took place in the days of Xisuthras,[12] the tenth King of the Chaldeans, and is of importance for comparison with the rendering of the Legend of the Deluge, as found on the Ninevite tablets, which follows immediately after.

The Legend Of The Deluge According To Berosus

"After the death of Ardates, his son Xisuthrus reigned eighteen sari. In his time happened a great Deluge; the history of which is thus described. The Deity, Cronus, appeared to him in a vision, and warned him that upon the 15th day of the month Daesius there would be a flood, by which mankind would be destroyed. He therefore enjoined him to write a history of the beginning, procedure and conclusion of all things; and to bury it in the city of the Sun at Sippara; and to build a vessel, and take with him into it his friends and relations; and to convey on board everything necessary to sustain life, together with all the different animals, both birds and quadrupeds, and trust himself fearlessly to the deep. Having asked the Deity, whither he was to sail? he was answered, 'To the Gods ': upon which he offered up a prayer for the good of mankind. He then obeyed the divine admonition; and built a vessel 5 stadia in length, and 2 in breadth. Into this he put everything which he had prepared; and last of all conveyed into it his wife, his children, and his friends. After the flood had been upon the earth, and was in time abated, Xisuthrus sent out birds from the vessel; which, not finding any food nor any place whereupon they might rest their feet, returned to him again. After an interval of some days, he sent them forth a second time; and they now returned with their feet tinged with mud. He made a trial a third time with these birds; but they returned to him no more: from whence he judged that the surface of the earth had appeared above the waters. He therefore made an opening in the vessel, and upon looking out found that it was stranded upon the side of some mountain; upon which he immediately quitted it with his wife, his daughter, and the pilot. Xisuthrus then paid his adoration to the earth, and, having constructed an altar, offered sacrifices to the gods, and, with those who had come out of the vessel with him, disappeared. They, who remained within, finding that their companions did not return, quitted the vessel with many lamentations, and called continually on the name of Xisuthrus. Him they saw no more; but they could distinguish his voice in the air, and could hear him admonish them to pay due regard to religion; and likewise informed them that it was upon account of his piety that be was translated to live with the gods; that his wife and daughter, and the pilot, had obtained the same honour. To this he added that they should return to Babylonia; and, it was ordained, search for the writings at Sippara, which they were to make known to mankind: moreover that the place, wherein they then were, was the land of Armenia. The rest having beard these words, offered sacrifices to the gods; and taking a circuit journeyed towards Babylonia." (Cory, *Ancient Fragments*, London, 1832, p. 26 *ff*.)

The Babylonian Legend Of The Deluge As Told To The Hero Gilgamish By His Ancestor Uta-Napishtim, Who Had Been Made Immortal By The Gods

The form of the Legend of the Deluge given below is that which is found on the Eleventh of the Series of Twelve Tablets in the Royal Library at Nineveh, which described the life and exploits of Gilgamish, an early king of the city of Erech. As we have seen above, the Legend of the Deluge has probably no original connection with the Epic of Gilgamish, but was introduced into it by the editors of the Epic at a comparatively late period, perhaps even during the reign of Ashur-bani-pal (B.C. 669-626).

A summary of the contents of the other Tablets of the Gilgamish Series is given in the following section of this short monograph.

It is therefore only necessary to state here that Gilgamish, who was horrified and almost beside himself when his bosom friend and companion Enkidu died, meditated deeply how he could escape death himself. He knew that his ancestor Uta-Napishtim a had become immortal, therefore he determined to set out for the place where Uta-Napishtim lived so that he might obtain from him the secret of immortality.

Guided by a dream, Gilgamish set out for the Mountain of the Sunset, and, after great toil and many difficulties, came to the shore of a vast sea. Here he met Ur-Shanabi, the boatman of Uta-Napishtim, who was persuaded to carry him in his boat over the "waters of death", and at length he landed on the shore of the country of Uta-Napishtim.

The immortal came down to the shore and asked the newcomer the object of his visit, and Gilgamish told him of the death of his great friend Enkidu, and of his desire to escape from death and to find immortality.

Uta-Napishtim having made to Gilgamish some remarks which seem to indicate that in his opinion death was inevitable,

1. Gilgamish[13] said unto him, to Uta-Napishtim the remote:

2. "I am looking at thee, Uta-Napishtim.

3. Thy person is not altered; even as am I so art thou.

4. Verily, nothing about thee is changed; even as am I so art thou.

5. A heart to do battle doth make thee complete,

6. Yet at rest (?) thou dost lie upon thy back.

7. How then hast thou stood the company of the gods and sought life?"

Thereupon Uta-Napishtim related to Gilgamish the Story of the Deluge, and the Eleventh Tablet continues thus

8. Uta-Napishtim said unto him, to Gilgamish:

9. "I will reveal unto thee, O Gilgamish, a hidden mystery,

10. And a secret matter of the gods I will declare unto thee.

11. Shurippak,[14] a city which thou thyself knowest,

12. On [the bank] of the river Puratti (Euphrates) is situated,

13. That city is old; and the gods [dwelling] within it

14. Their hearts induced the great gods to make a windstorm (*a-bu-bi*),[15]

15. There was their father Anu,

16. Their counsellor, the warrior Enlil,

17. Their messenger En-urta [and]

18. Their prince Ennugi.

19. Nin-igi-ku, Ea, was with them [in council] and

20. reported their word to a house of reeds."

[FIRST SPEECH OF EA TO UTA-NAPISHTIM WHO IS SLEEPING IN A REED HUT.]

21. O House of reeds, O House of reeds! O Wall. O Wall!

22. O House of reeds, hear! O Wall, understand!

23. O man of Shurippak, son of Ubar-Tutu,

24. Throw down the house, build a ship,

25. Forsake wealth, seek after life,

26. Hate possessions, save thy life,

27. Bring all seed of life into the ship.

28. The ship which thou shalt build,

29. The dimensions thereof shall be measured,

30. The breadth and the length thereof shall be the same.

31. Then launch it upon the ocean.

[UTA-NAPISHTIM'S ANSWER TO EA.]

32. I understood and I said unto Ea, my lord:

33. See, my lord, that which thou hast ordered,

34. I regard with reverence, and will perform it,

35. But what shall I say to the town, to the multitude, and to the
elders?

[SECOND SPEECH OF EA.]

36. Ea opened his mouth and spake

37. And said unto his servant, myself,

38. Thus, man, shalt thou say unto them:

39. Ill-will hath the god Enlil formed against me,

40. Therefore I can no longer dwell. in your city,

41. And never more will I turn my countenance upon-the soil of
Enlil.

42. I will descend into the ocean to dwell with my lord Ea.

43. But upon you he will rain riches

44. A catch of birds, a catch of fish

45. . . . an [abundant] harvest,

46. . . . the sender of . . .

47. . . . . shall make hail [to fall upon you].

[THE BUILDING OF THE SHIP.]

48. As soon as [something of dawn] broke . . .

[Lines 49-54 broken away.]

55. The child . . . brought bitumen,

56. The strong [man] . . . brought what was needed.

57. On the fifth day I laid down its shape.

58. According to the plan its walls were 10 *gar*, (*i.e.* 120 cubits) high,

59. And the width of its deck (?) was equally 10 *gar*.

60. I laid down the shape of its forepart and marked it out (?).

61. I covered (?) it six times.

62. . . . I divided into seven,

63. Its interior I divided into nine,

64. Caulking I drove into the middle of it.

65. I provided a steering pole, and cast in all that was needful.

66. Six *sar* of bitumen I poured over the hull (?),

67. Three *sar* of pitch I poured into the inside.

68. The men who bear loads brought three sar of oil,

69. Besides a sar of oil which the tackling (?) consumed,

70. And two sar of oil which the boatman hid.

71. I slaughtered oxen for the [work]people,

72. I slew sheep every day.

73. Beer, sesame wine, oil and wine

74. I made the people drink as if they were water from the river.

75. I celebrated a feast as if it had been New Year's Day.

76. I opened [a box of ointment], I laid my hands in unguent.

77. Before the sunset (?) the ship was finished.

78. [Since] . . . was difficult.

79. The shipbuilders brought the . . . of the ship, above and below,

80. . . . two-thirds of it.

[THE LOADING OF THE SHIP.]

81. With everything that I possessed I loaded it (*i.e.*, the ship).

82. With everything that I possessed of silver I loaded it.

83. With everything that I possessed of gold I loaded it.

84. With all that I possessed of all the seed of life I loaded it.

85. I made to go up into the ship all my family and kinsfolk,

86. The cattle of the field, the beasts of the field, all handicraftsmen I made them go up into it.

87. The god Shamash had appointed me a time (saying)

88. The sender of . . . . . will at eventide make a hail to fall;

89. Then enter into the ship and shut thy door.

90. The appointed time drew nigh;

91. The sender of . . . . . made a hail to fall at eventide.

92. I watched the aspect of the [approaching] storm,

93. Terror possessed me to look upon it,

94. I went into the ship and shut my door.

95. To the pilot of the ship, Puzur-Enlil the sailor

96. I committed the great house (*i.e.*, ship), together with the contents thereof.

[THE ABUBU (CYCLONE) AND ITS EFFECTS DESCRIBED.]

97. As soon as something of dawn shone in the sky

98. A black cloud from the foundation of heaven came up.

99. Inside it the god Adad thundered,

100. The gods Nabû and Sharru (*i.e.*, Marduk) went before,

101. Marching as messengers over high land and plain,

102. Irragal (Nergal) tore out the post of the ship,

103. En-urta went on, he made the storm to descend.

104. The Anunnaki[16] brandished their torches,

105. With their glare they lighted up the land.

106. The whirlwind (or, cyclone) of Adad swept up to heaven.

107. Every gleam of light was turned into darkness.

108. . . . . . . the land . . . . . as if had laid it waste.

109. A whole day long [the flood descended] . . .

110. Swiftly it mounted up . . . . . [the water] reached to the mountains

111. [The water] attacked the people like a battle.

112. Brother saw not brother.

113. Men could not be known (or, recognized) in heaven.

114. The gods were terrified at the cyclone.

115. They shrank back and went up into the heaven of Anu.

116. The gods crouched like a dog and cowered by the wall.

117. The goddess Ishtar cried out like a woman in travail.

118. The Lady of the Gods lamented with a sweet voice [saying]:

[ISHTAR'S LAMENT.]

119. May that former day be turned into mud,

120. Because I commanded evil among the company of the gods.

121. How could I command evil among the company of the gods,

122. Command battle for the destruction of my people?

123. Did I of myself bring forth my people

124. That they might fill the sea like little fishes?

[UTA-NAPISHTIM'S STORY CONTINUED.]

125. The gods, the Anunnaki wailed with her.

126. The gods bowed themselves, and sat down weeping.

127. Their lips were shut tight (in distress) . . .

128. For six days and nights

129. The wind, the storm raged, and the cyclone overwhelmed the land.

[THE ABATING OF THE STORM.]

130. When the seventh day came the cyclone ceased, the storm and battle

131. which had fought like an army.

132. The sea became quiet, the grievous wind went down, the cyclone ceased.

133. I looked on the day and voices were stilled,

134. And all mankind were turned into mud,

135. The land had been laid flat like a terrace.

136. I opened the air-hole and the light fell upon my cheek,

137. I bowed myself, I sat down, I cried,

138. My tears poured down over my cheeks.

139. I looked over the quarters of the world, (to] the limits of ocean.

140. At twelve points islands appeared.

141. The ship grounded on the mountain of Nisir.

142. The mountain of Nisir held the ship, it let it not move.

143. The first day, the second day, the mountain of Nisir held the ship and let it not move.

144. The third day, the fourth day, the mountain of Nisir held the ship and let it not move.

145. The fifth day, the sixth day, the mountain of Nisir held the ship and let it not move.

146. When the seventh day had come

147. I brought out a dove and let her go free.

148. The dove flew away and [then] came back;

149. Because she had no place to alight on she came back.

150. I brought out a swallow and let her go free.

151. The swallow flew away and [then] came back;

152. Because she had no place to alight on she came back.

153. 1 brought out a raven and let her go free.

154. The raven flew away, she saw the sinking waters.

155. She ate, she waded (?), she rose (?), she came not back.

[UTA-NAPISHTIM LEAVES THE SHIP.]

156. Then I brought out [everything] to the four winds and made a sacrifice;

157. I set out an offering on the peak of the mountain.

158. Seven by seven I set out the vessels,

159. Under them I piled reeds, cedarwood and myrtle (?).

160. The gods smelt the savour,

161. The gods smelt the sweet savour.

162. The gods gathered together like flies over him that sacrificed.

[SPEECH OF ISHTAR, LADY OF THE GODS.]

163 Now when the Lady of the Gods came nigh,

164. She lifted up the priceless jewels which Anu had made according to her desire, [saying]

165. O ye gods here present, as I shall never forget the sapphire jewels of my neck

166. So shall I ever think about these days, and shall forget them nevermore!

167. Let the gods come to the offering,

168. But let not Enlil come to the offering,

16q. Because he took not thought and made the cyclone,

170. And delivered my people over to destruction."

[THE ANGER OF ENLIL.]

171. Now when Enlil came nigh

172. He saw the ship; then was Enlil wroth

173. And he was filled with anger against the gods, the Igigi [saying]:[17]

174. Hath any being escaped with his life?

175. He shall not remain alive, a man among the destruction

[SPEECH OF EN-URTA.]

176. Then En-urta opened his mouth and spake

177. And said unto the warrior Enlil:

178. Who besides the god Ea can make a plan?

179. The god Ea knoweth everything that is done.

18o. The god Ea opened his mouth and spake

181. And said unto the warrior Enlil,

182. O Prince among the gods, thou warrior,

183. How, how couldst thou, not taking thought, make a cyclone?

184. He who is sinful, on him lay his sin,

185. He who transgresseth, on him lay his transgression.

186. But be merciful that [everything] be not destroyed be long-suffering that [man be not blotted out].

187. Instead of thy making a cyclone,

188. Would that the lion had come and diminished mankind.

189. Instead of thy making a cyclone

190. Would that the wolf had come and diminished mankind.

191. Instead of thy making a cyclone

192. Would that a famine had arisen and [laid waste] the land.

193. Instead of thy making a cyclone

194. Would that Irra (the Plague god) had risen up and [laid waste] the land.

195. As for me I have not revealed the secret of the great gods.

196. I made Atra-hasis to see a vision, and thus he heard the secret of the gods.

197. Now therefore take counsel concerning him.

[ENLIL DEIFIES UTA-NAPISHTIM AND HIS WIFE.]

198. Then the god Enlil went up into the ship,

199. He seized me by the hand and brought me forth.

200. He brought forth my wife and made her to kneel by my side.

201. He touched our brows, he stood between us, he blessed us [saying],

202. Formerly Uta-Napishtim was a man merely,

203. But now let Uta-Napishtim and his wife be like unto us gods.

204. Uta-Napishtim shall dwell afar off, at the mouth of the rivers.

[UTA-NAPISHTIM ENDS HIS STORY OF THE DELUGE.]

205. And they took me away to a place afar off, and made me to dwell at the mouth of the rivers.

The contents of the remainder of the text on the Eleventh Tablet of the Gilgamish Series are described on p. 54.

The Epic Of Gilgamish

The name of Gilgamish was formerly read "Izdubar," "Gizdubar," or "Gishdubar." He is probably referred to as {Greek Gílgamos} in Aelian, De Natura Animalium, XII, 23: (ed. Didot, Paris, 1858, p. 210).

The narrative of the life, exploits and travels of Gilgamish, king of Erech, filled Twelve Tablets which formed the Series called from the first three words of the First Tablet, SHA NAGBU IMURU, *i.e.*, "He who hath seen all things." The exact period of the reign of this king is unknown, but in the list of the Sumerian kingdoms he is fifth ruler in the Dynasty of Erech, which was considered the second dynasty to reign after the Deluge. He was said to have ruled for 126 years. The principal authorities for the Epic are the numerous fragments of the tablets that were found in the ruins of the Library of Nebo and the Royal Library of Ashur-bani-pal at Nineveh, and are now in the British Museum,[18] but very valuable portions of other and older versions (including some fragments of a Hittite translation) have now been recovered from various sources, and these contribute greatly to the reconstruction of the story. The contents of the Twelve Tablets may be briefly described thus—

THE FIRST TABLET.

The opening lines describe the great knowledge and wisdom of Gilgamish, who saw everything, learned everything, under stood everything, who probed to the bottom the hidden mysteries of wisdom, and who knew the history of everything that happened before the Deluge. He travelled far over sea and land, and performed mighty deeds, and then he cut upon a tablet of stone an account of all that he had done and suffered. He built the wall of Erech, founded the holy temple of E-Anna, and carried out other great architectural works. He was a semi-divine being, for his body was formed of the "flesh of the gods," and "two-thirds of him were god, and one-third was man," The description of his person is lost. As Shepherd (*i.e.*, King) of Erech he forced the

people to toil overmuch, and his demands reduced them to such a state
of misery that they cried out to the gods and begged them to create
some king who should control Gilgamish and give them deliverance
from him. The gods hearkened to the prayer of the men of Erech, and
they commanded the goddess Aruru to create a rival to Gilgamish. The
goddess agreed to do their bidding, and having planned in her mind
what manner of being she intended to make, she washed her hands, took
a piece of clay, cast it on the ground, and made a male creature like
the god En-urta. His body was covered all over with hair. The hair of
his head was long like that of a woman, and he wore clothing like that
of Sumuqan, the god of cattle. He was different in every way from the
people of the country, and his name was Enkidu. He lived in the forests
on the hills, ate herbs like the gazelle, drank with the wild cattle, and
herded with the beasts of the field. He was mighty in stature, invincible
in strength, and obtained complete mastery over all the creatures of the
forests in which he lived.

One day a certain hunter went out to snare game, and he dug
pit-traps and laid nets, and made his usual preparations for roping in his
prey. But after doing this for three days he found that his pits were filled
up and his nets smashed, and he saw Enkidu releasing the beasts that had
been snared. The hunter was terrified at the sight of Enkidu, and went
home hastily and told his father what he had seen and how badly he had
fared. By his father's advice he went to Erech, and reported to Gilgamish
what had happened. When Gilgamish heard his story he advised him
to act upon a suggestion which the hunter's father had already made,
namely that he should hire a harlot and take her out to the forest, so
that Enkidu might be ensnared by the sight of her beauty, and take up
his abode with her. The hunter accepted this advice, and having found
a harlot to help him in removing Enkidu from the forests, he set out
from Erech with her and in due course arrived at the forest where Enkidu
lived, and sat down by the place where the beasts came to drink.

On the second day when the beasts came to drink and Enkidu was with them, the woman carried out the instructions which the hunter had given her, and when Enkidu saw her cast aside her veil, he left his beasts and came to her, and remained with her for six days and seven nights. At the end of this period he returned to the beasts with which he had lived on friendly terms, but as soon as the gazelle winded him they took to flight, and the wild cattle disappeared into the woods. When Enkidu saw the beasts forsake him his knees gave way, and he could not run as of old; but when he came to himself he returned to the harlot. She spoke to him flattering words, and asked him why he wandered with the wild beasts in the desert, and then told him she wished to take him back with her to Erech, where Anu and Ishtar lived, and where the mighty Gilgamish reigned. Enkidu hearkened and the harlot then told him of the glories of Erech and of Gilgamish, who, she said, had been forewarned of Enkidu's coming by two dreams, which he had related to his divine mother, Nin-sun. These she had interpreted as foreshowing the approach of a strong and faithful friend.

THE SECOND TABLET.

Having related these dreams of Gilgamish, the harlot again urged Enkidu to go with her to Erech, and they set out together. On the way she brought him to a shepherds' village, where she instructed him how to eat the bread and beer which was set before him; for until then he had only sucked the milk of cattle. By virtue of eating and drinking this human fare Enkidu became a man instead of a beast, and, taking weapons, he hunted the lions and wolves which preyed upon the shepherds' flocks. A messenger from Gilgamish now appeared with a summons to the city. He announced that the king offered entertainment, but that he would expect the customary present from a stranger, and would exercise his privilege over the woman who accompanied him. The entrance of Enkidu into the city caused a general excitement, all being amazed at his surpassing strength and his conversion from savagery. The

first meeting of Gilgamish and Enkidu took place when the king came
in the night to claim his right to the strange woman. Enkidu violently
resisted him, and the two heroes in the doorway "grappled and snorted
(?) like bulls; they shattered the threshold, the wall quivered" in their
strife. Gilgamish was finally worsted, but the result of this combat was
that the two became fast friends and allies.

THE THIRD TABLET.

Owing to mutilation of the text this section begins obscurely, but it
seems that the harlot had deserted Enkidu, for he laments his association
with her. Gilgamish then opened to him his design to go on an
expedition to the Cedar Forest and fight with a fearful ogre named
Khumbaba, who had been appointed by the gods as warden of the forest.
Enkidu sought to dissuade his friend from this rash project, saying that
he himself, when he lived with the beasts, used to penetrate into the
skirts of the forest, where he had learned to dread the roaring breath
and flames emitted by Khumbaba. To this Gilgamish seems to have
replied that he must go to the Cedar Forest to fetch the wood he needed,
and when Enkidu still objected, he concluded with the reflection that
death was inevitable to mortals, and that he would therefore meet it in
a glorious enterprise which should win fame for him among his children
for ever. The craftsmen were then ordered to cast weapons for the pair,
and this they did, making gigantic axes and gold-ornamented swords, so
that each of the warriors was equipped with an armament weighing in all
ten talents. Attracted by these preparations, the people of Erech gathered
at the gate, and Gilgamish announced his project to the elders of the city,
who in turn sought to dissuade him, but in vain. Gilgamish commended
his life to the Sun-god, and the two put on their armour. The last words
of the elders were a warning to the king against rash presumption in
his own strength. Setting out on their journey, the two warriors first
visited the temple of Nin-sun, the divine mother of Gilgamish, who, at
the earnest prayer of her son, besought the Sun-god to prosper him on

his journey and in the fight against the ogre, and to bring him safely back to Erech. The latter part of this Tablet is missing.

THE FOURTH TABLET.

So much of this Tablet is missing that only a very general notion can be obtained of its contents. The two heroes had by now reached the Gate of the Forest wherein Khumbaba dwelt. Enkidu was amazed at the gigantic size and beauty of this gate, fashioned out of the timbers of the forest. When the text begins again, the two are found encouraging each other to their enterprise, and Gilgamish burst through the gate. Soon afterwards Enkidu was overcome either by sickness or by dread of the combat, and lay inert for twelve days, apparently as the result of evil dreams which had visited him. In his weakness he strove again to turn back from their desperate adventure, but again Gilgamish overcame his fear with encouragements.

THE FIFTH TABLET.

The two warriors were now in the forest, and this Tablet begins with a description of its wonders. They saw a straight road running between its tall cedars, along which Khumbaba trod; they saw also the mountain of the cedars, the dwelling of the gods, and the pleasant shade and perfume which the trees spread around. After this they seem to have fallen asleep, for Gilgamish is next found relating to Enkidu a dream which he had had: the two were standing together on the top of a mountain, when the peak fell away, leaving them unharmed. Enkidu interprets this as a forecast that they were to over-throw the gigantic Khumbaba. At the sixtieth league they stayed to rest, and Gilgamish besought the mountain to send him another dream. Falling asleep at once, he woke in terror at midnight and began to tell how he dreamed that the earth was darkened, amid loud roarings and flames of fire, which gradually died away. (This seems to be a description of a volcanic eruption, and some have thought that Khumbaba was the personification of a volcano known to the ancient Sumerians.) This dream too was interpreted by Enkidu, no doubt favourably, but nothing more remains of this Tablet before the end, when Khumbaba has been fought and defeated, and his head cut off. A fragment of another version shews that he was defeated by the help of the Sun-god, who sent eight evil winds against him on every side so that he could not move. Thus entrapped, he surrendered to Gilgamish and offered submission in return for his life. This Gilgamish was disposed to grant, but Enkidu warned him of the danger of letting the giant live.

THE SIXTH TABLET.

The scene now returns to Erech, whither the heroes returned after their glorious exploit. As Gilgamish was washing himself and dressing himself in splendid attire the goddess Ishtar saw his comeliness and desired him to be her lover, saying,

> Go to, Gilgamish, do thou be (my) bridegroom,
> Give me freely the fruit (of thy body).
> Be thou my husband, I will be thy wife,
> (So) will I make them yoke for thee a chariot of lapis-lazuli and gold,
> Its wheels of gold, and its horns of electrum.
> Every day shalt thou harness great mules thereto.
> Enter (then) our house with the perfume of cedar.
> When thou enterest our house
> Threshold and dais shall kiss thy feet,
> Beneath thee shall kings, lords and princes do homage,
> Bringing thee as tribute the yield of the mountains and plains,
> Thy she-goats shall bring forth abundantly, thy ewes bear twins,
> Thine asses shall be (each) as great as a mule,
> Thy horses in the chariot shall be famous for their swiftness,
> Thy mules in the yoke shall not have a peer.

In answer to this invitation, Gilgamish made a long speech, in which he reviewed the calamities of those who had been unfortunate enough to attract the love of the goddess. To be her husband would be a burdensome privilege, and her love was deceptive, a ruin that gave no shelter, a door that let in the storm, a crazy building, a pitfall, defiling pitch, a leaky vessel, a crumbling stone, a worthless charm, an ill-fitting shoe. "Who was ever thy lord that had advantage thereby? Come, I will unfold the tale of thy lovers." He refers to Tammuz, the lover of her youth, for whom year by year she causes wailing. Every creature that fell under her sway suffered mutilation or death; the bird's wings were broken, the lion destroyed, the horse driven to death with whip and spur. Her human lovers fared no better, for a shepherd, once her favourite, was turned by her into a jackal and torn by his own dogs, and Ishullanu, her father's gardener, was turned into a spider (?) because he refused her advances. "So, too," said Gilgamish, "would'st thou love me, and (then) make me like unto them."

Extract from the text of the Sixth Tablet of the Gilgamish Series (lines 50–70), containing a part of the speech which Gilgamish addressed to Ishtar in answer to her overtures to him. He reviles the goddess and reminds her of the death of Tammuz, and the sufferings of all the creatures that have been unfortunate enough to enter her service. From Rawlinson, *Cuneiform Inscriptions Western Asia*, Vol. IV, Plate 41, col. 2. (K. 2589.)

When Ishtar heard these words she was filled with rage, and went up to heaven, and complained to Anu her father and Antu her mother that Gilgamish had blasphemed her, and revealed all her iniquitous deeds. Anu replied, in effect, that it was her own fault, but she insisted in the request that he should create a heavenly bull to destroy Gilgamish. This he finally agreed to do, and the bull appeared before the citizens of Erech, and destroyed one, two and three hundred men who were sent out against him. At length Enkidu and Gilgamish attacked the bull themselves, and after a hard fight: the details of which are lost, they slew him, and offered his heart together with a libation to the Sun-god. As soon as Ishtar heard of the bull's death she rushed out on the battlements of the wall of Erech and cursed Gilgamish for destroying her bull. When Enkidu heard what Ishtar said, he tore out the member of the bull and threw it before the goddess, saying, "Could I but get it at thee, I would serve thee like him; I would hang his it entrails about thee." Then Ishtar gathered together all her temple-women and harlots, and with them made lamentation over the member of the bull.

And Gilgamish called together the artisans of Erech, who came and marvelled at the size of the bull's horns, for each of them was in bulk equal to 30 *minas* of lapis-lazuli, their thickness two finger-breadths, and together they contained six *kur* measures of oil. These Gilgamish dedicated in the temple of his god Lugalbanda, to hold the god's unguent, and, having made his offering, he and Enkidu washed their hands in the Euphrates, took their way back to the city, and rode through the streets of Erech, the people thronging round to admire them. Gilgamish put forth a question to the people, saying

Who is splendid among men?
Who is glorious among heroes?
And the answer was:

[Gilgamish] is splendid among men,

[Enkidu] is glorious among heroes.

Gilgamish made a great feast in his palace, and after it all lay down to sleep. Enkidu also slept and had a vision, so he rose up and related it to Gilgamish.

THE SEVENTH TABLET.

From fragments of a version of the Gilgamish Epic translated into the Hittite language, which have more recently been discovered, it is possible to gain some notion of the contents of this Tablet, the earlier part of which is almost entirely missing from the Assyrian version. It appears that Enkidu beheld in his dream the gods Enlil, Ea, and the Sun-god taking counsel together. Enlil was greatly incensed at the exploits of Gilgamish and Enkidu, and had resolved that Enkidu must die, though Gilgamish might be spared. This was finally decreed, in spite of the attempted opposition of the Sun-god. In consequence Enkidu soon afterwards fell sick, though nothing is preserved concerning the circumstances of this. But he seems to have attributed his misfortune for some reason to the harlot who had first brought him to Erech, for he is found heaping curses upon her. While he thus spoke the Sun-god heard him, and, calling from heaven, rebuked him for ingratitude to the woman, who had taught him all the ways of civilized life and had been the means of introducing him to Gilgamish, by whom he had been raised to great place and would be given signal honours at his death. Admonished thus, Enkidu repented of his anger and now bestowed as many blessings on the harlot as he had before uttered curses. He then lay down again, with sickness heavy upon him, and dreamed a dream which he told to Gilgamish. He saw a monster with lion's claws which attacked and overcame him, and led him away to the Underworld, where he saw the miserable plight of the dead inhabitants, and ancient kings now acting as servants, and priests and sages who served before Ereshkigal, the queen of Hades. How the dream ended, and how Enkidu died, is unknown, for the text breaks off here.

THE EIGHTH TABLET.

This Tablet was entirely occupied by a description of the mourning of Gilgamish over his dead companion. He lamented to himself, and lamented to the elders of the city, recalling how they had together overthrown Khumbaba, and slain the heavenly bull, and shared in many another exploit. Repeating the words of the Sun-god in the preceding Tablet, he promised that he would cause all his subjects to join with himself in the lament for Enkidu. The funeral honours seem to have been described in the latter part of the Tablet, which is missing.

THE NINTH TABLET.

In bitter grief Gilgamish wandered about the country uttering lamentations for his beloved companion, Enkidu. As he went about he thought to himself,

"I myself shall die, and shall not I then be as Enkidu?
Sorrow hath entered into my soul,
Because I fear death do I wander over the country."

His fervent desire was to escape from death, and remembering that his ancestor Uta-Napishtim, the son of Ubara-Tutu, had become deified and immortal, Gilgamish determined to set out for the place where he lived in order to obtain from him the secret of immortality. Where Uta-Napishtim lived was unknown to Gilgamish, but he seems to have made up his mind that he would have to face danger in reaching the place, for he says, "I will set out and travel quickly. I shall reach the defiles in the mountains by night, and if I see lions, and am terrified at them, I shall lift up my head and appeal to the Moon-god, and to (Ishtar, the Lady of the Gods), who is wont to hearken to my prayers." After Gilgamish set out to go to the west he was attacked either by men or animals, but he overcame them and went on until he arrived at

Mount Mashu, where it would seem the sun was thought both to rise and to set. The approach to this mountain was guarded by Scorpion-men, whose aspect was so terrible that the mere sight of it was sufficient to kill the mortal who beheld them; even the mountains collapsed under the glance of their eyes. When Gilgamish saw the Scorpion-men he was smitten with fear, and under the influence of his terror the colour of his face changed, and he fell prostrate before them. Then a Scorpion-man cried out to his wife, saying, "The body of him that cometh to us is the flesh of the gods," and she replied, "Two-thirds of him is god, and the other third is man." The Scorpion-man then received Gilgamish kindly, and warned him that the way which he was about to travel was full of danger and difficulty. Gilgamish told him that he was in search of his ancestor, Uta-Napishtim, who had been deified and made immortal by the gods, and that it was his intention to go to him to learn the secret of immortality. The Scorpion-man in answer told him that it was impossible for him to continue his journey through that country, for no man had ever succeeded in passing through the dark region of that mountain, which required twelve double-hours to traverse. Nothing dismayed, Gilgamish set out on the road through the mountains, and the darkness increased in density every hour, but he struggled on, and at the end of the twelfth hour he arrived at a region where there was bright daylight, and he entered a lovely garden, filled with trees loaded with luscious fruits, and he saw the "tree of the gods." Here the Sun-god called to him that his quest must be in vain, but Gilgamish replied that he would do anything to escape death.

THE TENTH TABLET.

In the region to which Gilgamish had come stood the palace or fortress of the goddess Siduri, who was called the "hostess," or "ale-wife," and to this he directed his steps with the view of obtaining help to continue his journey. The goddess wore a veil and sat upon a throne by the side of the sea, and when she saw him coming towards her palace, travel-stained and clad in the ragged skin of some animal, she thought that he might prove an undesirable visitor, and so ordered the door of her palace to be closed against him. But Gilgamish managed to obtain speech with her, and having asked her what ailed her, and why she had closed her door, he threatened to smash the bolt and break down the door. In answer Siduri said to him:—

"Why is thy vigour wasted? Thy face is bowed down,

Thine heart is sad, thy form is dejected,

And there is lamentation in thy heart."

And she went on to tell him that he had the appearance of one who had travelled far, that he was a painful sight to look upon, that his face was burnt, and finally seems to have suggested that he was a runaway trying to escape from the country. To this Gilgamish replied:—

Nay, my vigour is not wasted, my face not bowed down,

My heart not sad, my form not dejected."

And then he told the goddess that his ill-looks and miserable appearance were due to the fact that death had carried off his dear friend Enkidu, the "panther of the desert," who had traversed the mountains with him and had helped him to overcome Khumbaba in the cedar forest, and to slay the bull of heaven, Enkidu his dear friend who had fought with lions and killed them, and who had been with him in all his difficulties; and, he added, "I wept over him for six days and nights . . . . before I would let him be buried." Continuing his narrative, Gilgamish said to Siduri:

"I was horribly afraid . . .

I was afraid of death, and therefore I wander over the country.

The fate of my friend lieth heavily upon me,

Therefore am I travelling on a long journey through the country.

The fate of my friend lieth heavily upon me,

Therefore am I travelling on a long journey through the country.

How is it possible for me to keep silence? How is it possible for me to cry out?

My friend whom I loved hath become like the dust.
Enkidu, my friend whom I loved hath become like the dust.
Shall not I myself also be obliged to lay me down
And never again rise up to all eternity?"

To this complaint the ale-wife replied that the quest of eternal life was vain, since death was decreed to mankind by the gods at the time of creation. She advised him, therefore, to enjoy all mortal pleasures while life lasted and to abandon his hopeless journey. But Gilgamish still persisted, and asked how he might reach Uta-Napishtim, for thither he was determined to go, whether across the ocean or by land.

Then the ale-wife answered and said to Gilgamish:

"There never was a passage, O Gilgamish,
And no one, who from the earliest times came hither, hath crossed the sea.
The hero Shamash (the Sun-god) hath indeed crossed the sea, but who besides him could do so?
The passage is hard, and the way is difficult,
And the Waters of Death which bar its front are deep.
If, then, Gilgamish, thou art able to cross the sea,
When thou arrivest at the Waters of Death what wilt thou do?"

Siduri then told Gilgamish that Ur-Shanabi, the boatman of Uta-Napishtim, was in the place, and that he should see him, and added:

"If it be possible cross with him, and if it be impossible turn back."

Gilgamish left the goddess and succeeded in finding Ur-Shanabi, the boatman, who addressed to him words similar to those of Siduri quoted above. Gilgamish answered him as he had answered Siduri, and then asked him for news about the road to Uta-Napishtim. In reply Ur-Shanabi told him to take his axe and to go down into the forest and cut a number of poles 60 cubits long; Gilgamish did so, and when he returned with them he went up into the boat with Ur-Shanabi, and they made a voyage of one month and fifteen days; on the third day they reached the [limit of the] Waters of Death, which Ur-Shanabi told

Gilgamish not to touch with his hand. Meanwhile, Uta-Napishtim had seen the boat coming and, as something in its appearance seemed strange to him, he went down to the shore to see who the newcomers were. When he saw Gilgamish he asked him the same questions that Siduri and Ur-Shanabi had asked him, and Gilgamish answered as he had answered them, and then went on to tell him the reason for his coming. He said that he had determined to go to visit Uta-Napishtim, the remote, and had -therefore journeyed far, and that in the course of his travels he had passed over difficult mountains and crossed the sea. He had not succeeded in entering the house of Siduri, for she had caused him to be driven from her door on account of his dirty, ragged, and travel-stained apparel. He had eaten birds and beasts of many kinds, the lion, the panther, the jackal, the antelope, mountain goat, etc., and, apparently, had dressed himself in their skins.

A break in the text makes it impossible to give the opening lines of Uta-Napishtim's reply, but he mentions the father and mother of Gilgamish, and in the last twenty lines of the Tenth Tablet he warns Gilgamish that on earth there is nothing permanent, that Mammitum, the arranger of destinies, has settled the question of the death and life of man with the Anunnaki, and that none may find out the day of his death or escape from death.

THE ELEVENTH TABLET.

The story of the Deluge as told by Uta-Napishtim to Gilgamish has already been given on pp. 31-40, and we therefore pass on to the remaining contents of this Tablet. When Uta-Napishtim had finished the story of the Deluge, he said to Gilgamish, "Now, as touching thyself; who will gather the gods together for thee, so that thou mayest find the life which thou seekest? Come now, do not lay thyself down to sleep for six days and seven nights." But in spite of this admonition, as soon as Gilgamish had sat down, drowsiness overpowered him and he fell fast asleep. Uta-Napishtim, seeing that even the mighty hero Gilgamish could not resist falling asleep, with some amusement drew the attention of his wife to the fact, but she felt sorry for the tired man, and suggested that he should take steps to help him to return to his home. In reply Uta-Napishtim told her to bake bread for him, and she did so, but she noted by a mark on the house-wall each day that he slept. On the seventh day, when she took the loaf Uta-Napishtim touched Gilgamish, and the hero woke up with a start, and admitted that he had been overcome with sleep, and made incapable of movement thereby.

Still vexed with the thought of death and filled with anxiety to escape from it, Gilgamish asked his host what he should do and where he should go to effect his object. By Uta-Napishtim's advice, he made an agreement with Ur-Shanabi the boatman, and prepared to re-cross the sea on his way home. But before he set out on his way Uta-Napishtim told him of the existence of a plant which grew at the bottom of the sea, and apparently led Gilgamish to believe that the possession of it would confer upon him immortality. Thereupon Gilgamish tied heavy stones [to his feet], and let himself down into the sea through an opening in the floor of the boat. When he reached the bottom of the sea, he saw the plant and plucked it, and ascended into the boat with it. Showing it to Ur-Shanabi, he told him that it was a most marvellous plant, and that it would enable a man to obtain his heart's desire. Its name was "Shîbu issahir amelu," *i.e.*, "The old man becometh young [again]," and Gilgamish declared that he would "eat of it in order to recover his lost youth," and that he would take it home to his fortified city of Erech. Misfortune, however, dogged his steps, and the plant never reached Erech, for whilst Gilgamish and Ur-Shanabi were on their way back to Erech they passed a pool the water of which was very cold, and Gilgamish dived into it and took a bath. Whilst there a serpent discovered the whereabouts of the plant through its smell and swallowed it. When Gilgamish saw what had happened he cursed aloud, and sat down and wept, and the tears coursed down his cheeks as he lamented over the waste of his toil, and the vain expenditure of his heart's blood, and his failure to do any good for himself. Disheartened and weary he struggled on his way with his friend, and at length they arrived at the fortified city of Erech.[12]

Then Gilgamish told Ur-Shanabi to jump up on the wall and examine the bricks from the foundations to the battlements, and see if the plans which he had made concerning them had been carried out during his absence.

THE TWELFTH TABLET.

The text of the Twelfth Tablet is very defective, but it seems certain that Gilgamish, having failed in his quest for eternal life, could now think of nothing better than to know the worst by calling up the ghost of Enkidu and enquiring of him as to the condition of the dead in the Under-world. He therefore asked the priests what precautions should be taken in order to prevent a ghost from haunting one, and, being informed of these, he purposely did everything against which he had been warned, so that the ghosts might come about him. This, however, failed to bring Enkidu, so Gilgamish prayed to the god Enlil that he should raise him up, but Enlil made no reply. Next Gilgamish prayed to the Moon-god, but again his prayer was ignored. He then appealed to the god Ea, who, taking pity on him, ordered the warrior-god Nergal to open a hole in the earth. Out of this the ghost of Enkidu rose "like a wind," and the two friends embraced again. Gilgamish at once began eagerly to question the ghost about the condition of the dead, but Enkidu was loath to answer, for he knew that what he must reveal would only cause his friend dejection. But the last lines of the Tablet tell the lot of those who have died in various circumstances; though some who have been duly buried are in better case, the fate of others who have none to pay them honour is miserable, for they are reduced to feeding upon dregs and scraps of food thrown into the street.

Plates

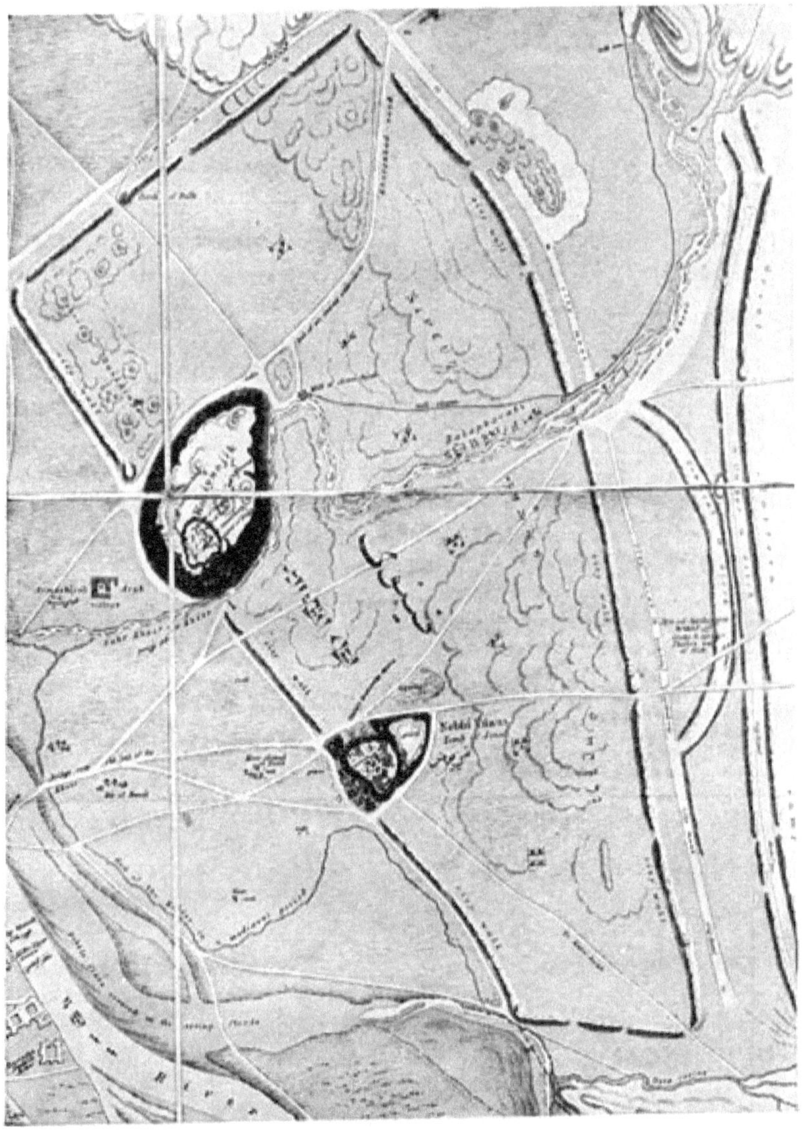

Plan of the ruins of the walls, temples and palaces of Nineveh, showing the course of the River Khausur, and the great protective ditches outside the eastern wall. The southern mound (Nabi Yûnis) contains the ruins of palaces, etc., built by Sargon II, Sennacherib and Esarhaddon, and the northern mound (Kuyûnjik) the Palaces and Library of Ashur-bani-pal, the Library of Nebo, etc. *From the drawing made by the late Commander Felix Jones, I.N.*

Baked clay cylinder of Sennacherib, King of Assyria, from B.C. 705 to 681, inscribed with an account of eight campaigns of the king, including the capture and sack of Babylon, the invasion of Palestine, and the siege of Jerusalem; it is dated in the eponymy of Bel-imurani, *i.e.*, B.C. 691. B.M. No. 91,032. This cylinder was found among the ruins of a palace of Sennacherib under the mound of Nabi Yûnis, and was bought by Colonel J. Taylor, Consul-General of Baghdâd in 1830, from whose representatives it was bought by the Trustees of the British Museum in 1855.

Baked clay six-sided cylinder, inscribed with the Annals of Esarhaddon, King of Assyria from B.C. 681–668. B.M. No. 91,028. This cylinder was found in the ruins of the palace of Esarhaddon, under the mound of Nabi Yûnis, and had been "used as a candlestick by a respectable Turcoman family living in the village on the mound near the tomb of the prophet [Jonah]." The grease marks from the candles are still visible on it. It was acquired by Sir Henry Layard and presented by him to the British Museum in 1848.

1
[Bu. 89.4-26. 11]
2
[Bu. 91. 5-9. 14]
3

Specimens of Tablets from Nineveh.
1. Astrological report concerning divinations of the Moon.
2. Astrological report concerning the Moon and Mercury.
3. Prayers of Ashur-bani-pal to Nebo.

1
[BU. 91. 5-9. 221]
2
3
4
[81. 7-27. 199]
[81. 7-27. 199]

Specimens of Tablets from Nineveh.
1. Part of a mythological legend concerning early Babylonian rulers.
2. Assyrian letter.
3 and 4. Letter and envelope from Ashur-ritsûa to an official.

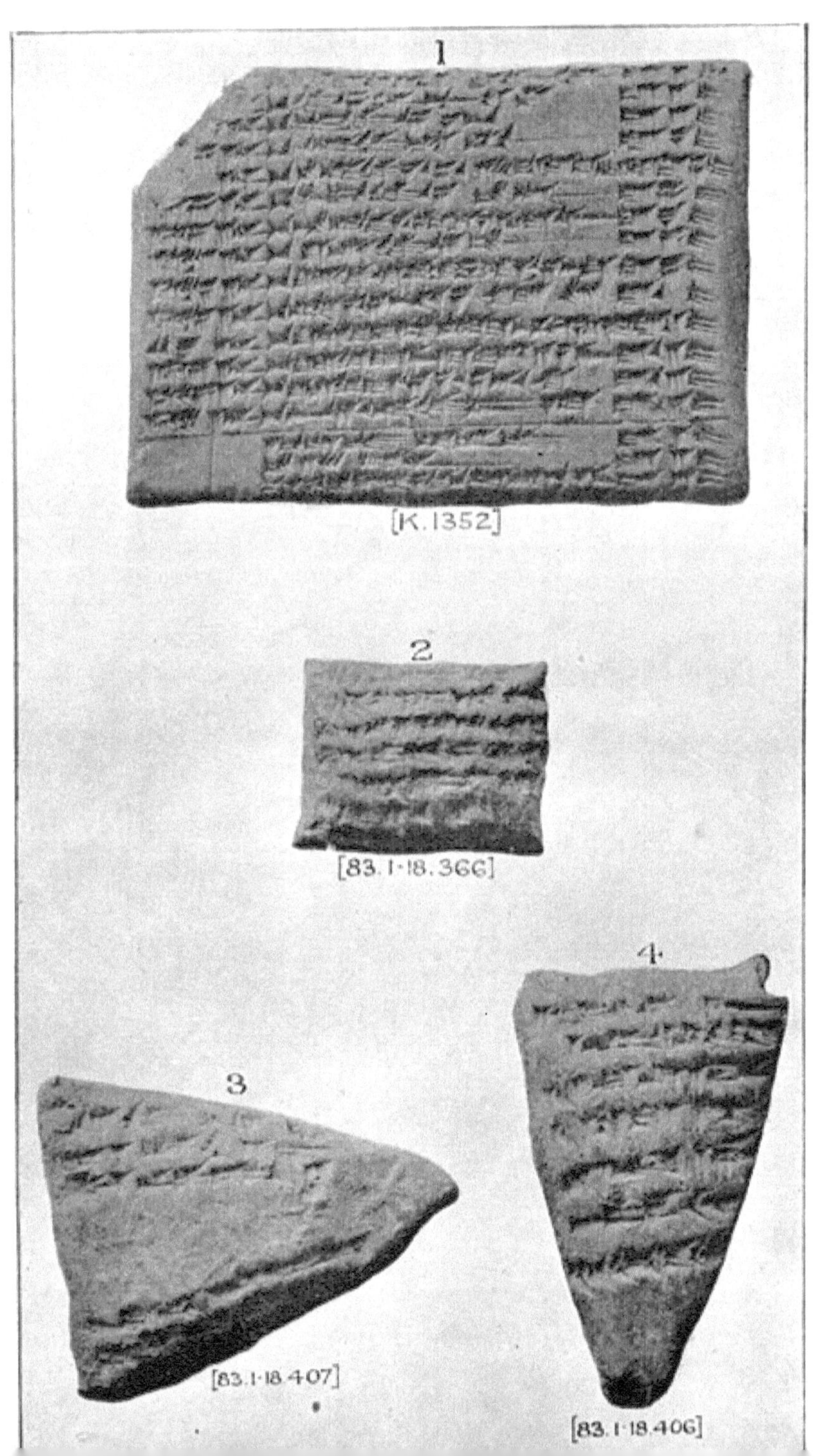
1
[K.1352]
2
[83.1.18.366]
4
3
[83.1.18.407]
[83.1.18.406]

Specimens of Tablets from Nineveh.
1. Catologue of Omen tablets, giving the first line of each.
2. Contract tablet, written B.C. 675.
3. Contract tablet, with the impression of a seal; written B.C. 693.
4. Contract tablet, written B.C. 686.

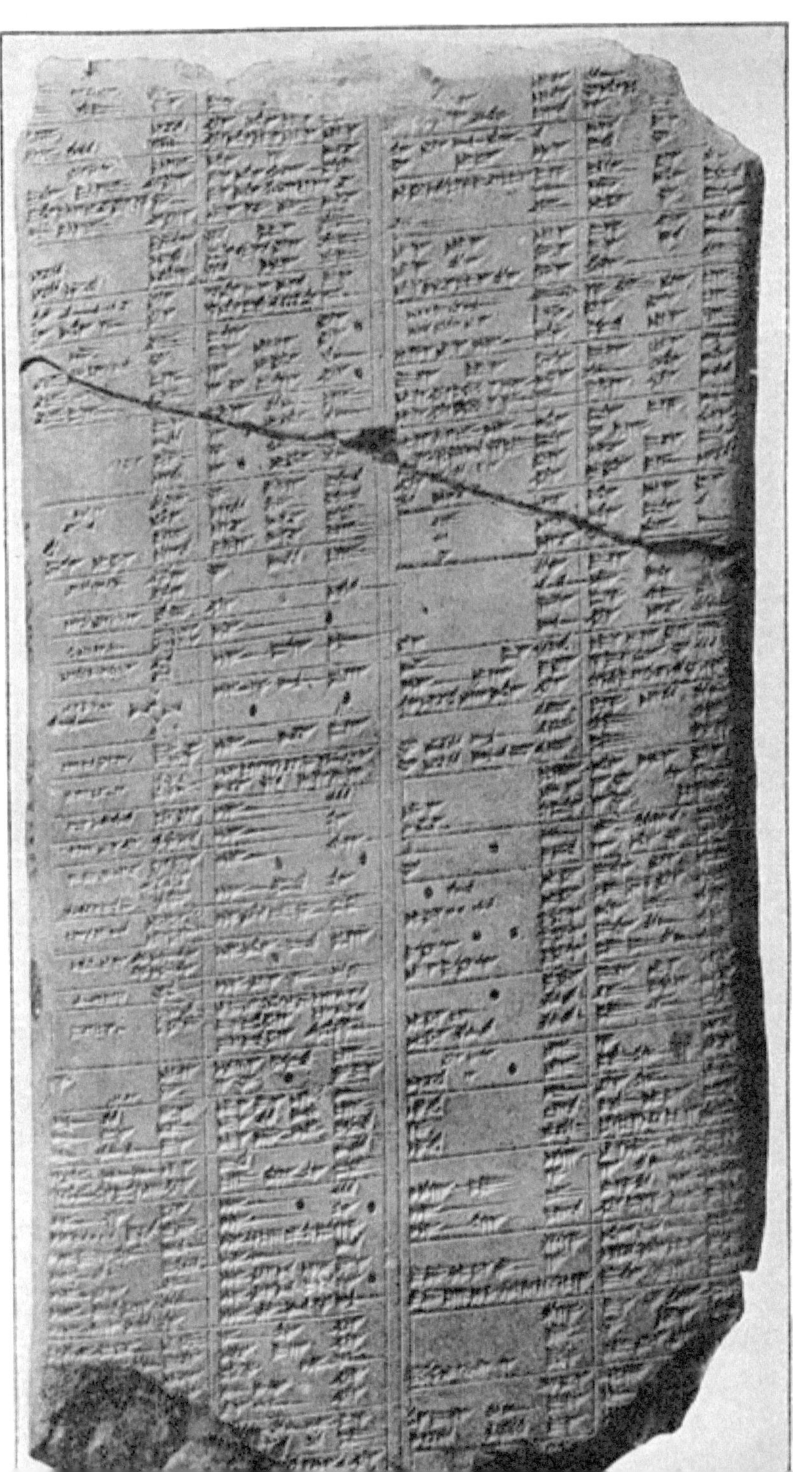

Specimen of Tablets from Nineveh.
Explanatory List of Words with glosses.

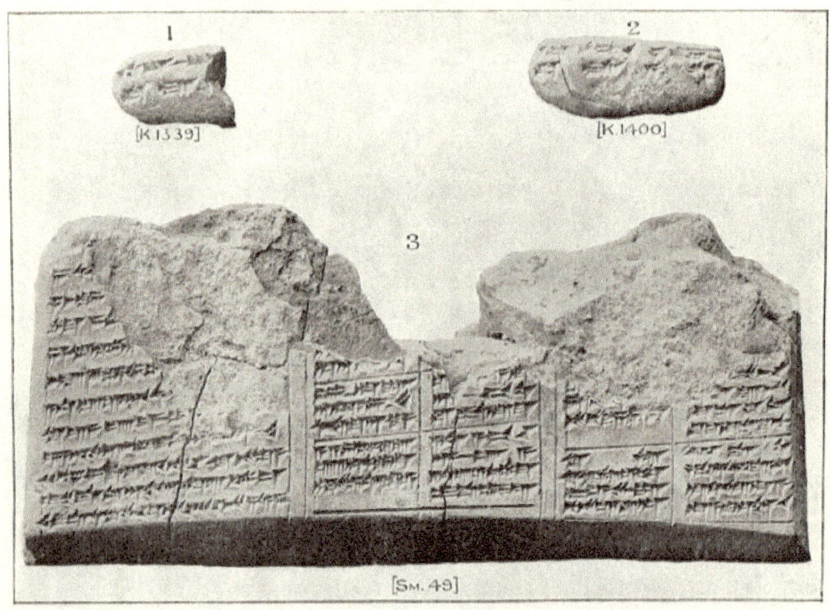

Specimens of Tablets from Nineveh.

1. Label, inscribed with the title of a series of strological forecasts.

2. Label, inscribed with the title of a series of omens.

3. Part of a text containing grammatical paradigms.

Baked clay ten-sided cylinder inscribed with a description of the most
important events of the reign of Ashur-bani-pal, king of Assyria, B.C.

668–626, and an account of the building operations which he carried on in Nineveh. B.M. No. 91,026. This cylinder was discovered in a chamber in one of the main walls of the palace of Ashur-bani-pal at Nineveh by Mr. Hormuzd Rassam in 1878.

Scene on bas-relief from a chamber in the palace of Ashur-bani-pal at Nineveh, in which the king is represented standing before a table of offerings and a divine symbol and pouring out a libation over a group of dead lions. Assyrian Saloon, No. 118.

[K. 47]

Tablet from the Temple of Nebo with Colophon.
Astrological Omens concerning cities.

[K. 7000]

Tablet from the Temple of Nebo with Colophon.

Forecasts which formed the Fourth Tablet of the Series

The Eleventh Tablet of the Gilgamish Series containing the Story of the Deluge as told to Gilgamish by his deified ancestor Uta-Napishtim, an antediluvian king of Erech. A portion of one end of the tablets was vitrified when Ashur-bani-pal's palace and the Librrary of Nebo were destroyed by fire. From the Library of the Temple of Nebo. Size, seven-eighths of the original. K. 3321 + S. 1881.

Portion of another copy of the Story of the Deluge, from a tablet which probably belonged to the Palace of Ashur-bani-pal at Nineveh. Photograph one-seventh larger than the original. K. 3375.

Note

The Trustees of the British Museum have published large selections of cuneiform texts from the cylinders, tablets, etc., that were found in the ruins of Nineveh by Layard, Rassam, Smith and others, in the following works:—

CUNEIFORM INSCRIPTIONS OF WESTERN ASIA. Vol. 1. 1861. Fol. I*l*. (Out of print.)

—————————Vol. II. 1866. Fol. I*l*. (Out of print.)

—————————Vol. 111. 1870. Fol. I*l*.

—————————Vol. IV. Second edition. 1891. Fol. I*l*. (Out of print.)

—————————Vol. V. Plates I-XXXV. 1880. Fol. 10s. 6d. (Out of print.)

—————————Vol. V. Plates XXXVI-LXX. 1884. Fol. 10s. 6d. (Out of print.)

—————————Vol. V. Plates I-LXX. Lithographed reprint 1909. Fol. I*l*. 7s.

INSCRIPTIONS FROM ASSYRIAN MONUMENTS. 1851. Fol. I*l*.. 1s.

CUNEIFORM TEXTS FROM BABYLONIAN TABLETS, &C., IN THE BRITISH MUSEUM. Parts I-V, VII-XXIII, XXV, XXVII-XXXIV. 50 plates each. 1896-1914. 7s. 6d. each.

—————————Part VI. 49 plates. 1898. 7s. 6d.

—————————Part XXIV. 50 plates. 1908. Fol. 10s.

—————————Part XXVI. 54 plates. 1909. Fol. 12s.

—————————Part XXXV. 50 plates. 1920. 12s.

—————————Part XXXVI. 50 plates. 1921. 18s.

————————Parts XXXVII, XXXIX. 50 plates each. 1924, 1926. 15s. each.

————————Parts XXXVIII, XL. 50 plates each. 19-25, 1928. 16s. each.

ANNALS OF THE KINGS OF ASSYRIA. Cuneiform texts with transliterations and translations. Vol. I. 1903. 4to. 1*l.*

CATALOGUE OF THE CUNEIFORM TABLETS IN THE KOUYUNJIK COLLECTION. Vol. I. 8vo. 1889. 15s.

——————Vol. II. 1891. 15s.

——————Vol. III. 1894. 13s.

——————Vol. IV. 1896. 1*l.*

——————Vol. V. 1899. 1*l.* 3s.

——————Supplement 8vo. 1914. 1*l.*

Footnotes

[←1]

It has recently been suggested, as a result of careful examination of the site, that the Tigris never actually flowed under the city wall. (R. C. Thompson, *A Century of Exploration at Nineveh*, p. 122 ff.)

[←2]

A group of Sumerian signs for "library" is ### (*girginakku*), and these seem to mean "collection of tablets."

[←3]

For a description of the ruins of this temple, see R. C. Thompson, *A Century of Exploration at Nineveh*, pp. 67-79

[←4]

These bas-reliefs show that lions were kept in cages in Nineveh and let out to be killed by the King with his own hand. There seems to be an allusion to the caged lions by Nahum (ii, 11), who says, "Where is the dwelling of the lions, and the feeding place of the young lions, where the lion, *even* the old lion, walked, and the lion's whelp, and none made *them* afraid?"

[←5]

K. 1352 is a, good specimen of a catalogue (see p. 10); K. 1400 and K. 1539 are labels (see p. 12)

[←6]

Or, probably better. "Thy lordship is beyond compare, O king the gods, Ashur."

[←7]

For a full description of the general contents of the two great Libraries of Nineveh. see Bezold, Catalogue of the Cuneiform Tablets of the Kouyûnjik Collection, Vol. V, London, 1899, p. xviii *ff.*; and King, *Supplement*, London, 1914, p. xviii *ff*

[←8]

Smith, *Assyrian Discoveries*, London, 1875, p. 97

[←9]

Published by Scheil in Maspero's *Recueil*, Vol. XX, p. 5.5 *ff.*, and again by Clay, *A Hebrew Deluge Story in Cuneiform*, Plates I, II.

[←10]

The text is published by A. Poebel with transcription, commentary, etc., in *Historical Texts*, Philadelphia, 1914, and *Historical and Grammatical Texts*, Philadelphia, 1914

[←11]
Budge, *The Book of the Cave of Treasures*, pp. i 12 *ff.*

[←12]

This is a Greek form of Zisudra, the name of the last king before the Flood, according to the Sumerian tradition

[←13]

A transcript of the cuneiform text by George Smith, who was the first to translate it, will be found in Rawlinson, *Cuneiform inscriptions of Western Asia*, Vol. IV, Plates 50 and 51: and a transcript, with transliteration and translation by the late Prof. L. W. King, is given in his *First Steps in Assyrian*, London, 1898, p. x61 *ff.* The latest translation of the whole poem is by R. C. Thompson, *The Epic of Gilgamish*, whose arrangement of the text is adopted in the following pages.

[←14]

The site of this very ancient city is marked by the mounds of Fârah, near the Shatt al-Kâr, which is probably the old bed of the river Euphrates; many antiquities belonging to the earliest period of the rule of the Sumerians have been found there

[←15]
Like the habûb of modern times, a sort of cyclone

[←16]
The star-gods of the southern sky

[←17]

The star-gods of the northern heaven

[←18]

The greater number of these have been collected, grouped and published by Haupt, *Das Babylonische Nimrodepos*, Leipzig, 1884 and 1891; and see his work on the Twelfth Tablet in *Beiträge zur Assyriologie*, Vol. I, p. 49 *ff*

[←19]

The city of Erech was the second of the four cities which, according to Genesis x, 10, were founded by Nimrod, the son of Cush, the "mighty hunter before the Lord. And the beginning of his kingdom was Babel, and Erech and Accad, and Calneh, in the land of Shinar." The Sumerians and Babylonian called the city "UNU KI,"; the first sign means "dwelling" or "habitation," and the second "land, country," etc.. and we may understand this as meaning the "dwelling" *par excellence* of some god, probably Anu. The site of Erech is well known, and is marked by the vast ruins which the Arabs call "Warkah," or Al-Warkah. These lie in 31° 19' N. Lat. and 45° 40' E. Long., and are about four miles from the Euphrates, on the left or east bank of the river. Sir W. K. Loftus carried out excavations on the site in 1849-52, and says that the external walls of sun-dried brick enclosing the main portion of the ruins form an irregular circle five and a-half miles in circumference; in places they are from 40 to 50 feet in height, and they seem to have been about 20 feet thick. The turrets on the wall were semi-oval in shape and about 50 feet apart. The principal ruin is that of the Ziggurat, or temple tower, which in 1850 was 100 feet high and 206 feet square. Loftus calls it "Buwáriya," *i.e.*, "reed mats," because reed mats were used in its construction, but *búriyah*, "rush mat," is a Persian not Arabic word, and the name is more probably connected with the Arabic "Bawâr," *i.e.*, "ruin," "place of death," etc. This tower stood in a courtyard which was 350 feet long and 270 feet wide. The next large ruin is that which is called "Waswas" (plur. Wasâwis"), *i.e.*, "large stone." The "Waswas" referred to was probably the block of columnar basalt which Loftus and Mr. T. K. Lynch found projecting through the soil; on it was sculptured the figure of a warrior, and the stone itself was regarded as a talisman by the natives. This ruin is 246 feet long, 174 feet wide and 80 feet high. On three sides of it are terraces of different elevations, but the south-west side presents a perpendicular façade, at one place 23 feet in height. For further details *see* Loftus, *Chaldea and Susiana*, London, 1857, p. 159 *ff.* Portions of the ruins of Warkah were excavated by German archaeologists in 1912. and this work was resumed in 1928

www.ingramcontent.com/pod-product-compliance
Lightning Source LLC
Chambersburg PA
CBHW031439130726
47989CB00003B/1215